NO TIME FOR GOOD REASONS

The publication of this book is supported
by a grant from the National Endowment for
the Arts in Washington, D.C., a Federal agency.

no time for good reasons

brendan galvin

university of pittsburgh press

Library of Congress Cataloging in Publication Data

Galvin, Brendan.
  No time for good reasons.

  (Pitt poetry series)
  Poems.
  I. Title.
PS3557.A44N6   811'.5'4   74-4091
ISBN 0-8229-5250-5

Acknowledgment is made to the following publications in which some of these poems first appeared: *The American Review, College English, Concerning Poetry, Critical Quarterly, The Dragonfly, Epoch, Falmouth Review, Harper's, The Hudson Review, Long Island Review, The Malahat Review, Monmouth Review, The Narrow Land, The New York Times, Nimrod, Northwest Review, The Ohio Review, Poetry Northwest, Prairie Schooner, The Salt Farm, Shankpainter,* and *Voices from Earth.*

"When You Go," "Hitchhiker," "Inversions of Summer," and "The Last Day of October" are reprinted from *The Massachusetts Review,* ©1971, The Massachusetts Review, Inc.

"The Bats" appeared originally in *The New Yorker.*

When You Go

for Ellen

When you go
for only an hour or two,
this house shifts
on winter paws and drifts

toward animal sleep. Calm
as the dark oak
held in the palm
of snow, I wake

to flakes that swim
the delicate, branched
system
of my head.

Let the long barns keep
their harvest of perfect sleep.

Contents

one

The Man with a Hole Through His Chest

Point Barrow Eskimo wood carving

He did it because the wind
pushed him around. When he set out
to walk to the dawn
it shoved him into the sunset;
getting inside, it startled thoughts
that were sleeping like leaves.
So he let it out,
made a place for it to go through.

Now an ear is closing,
tired of the wind's secrets.
One eye is frozen open
on the white absence of friends
while the other grows teeth,
tunneling into its brow.
Below stubborn nostrils
other teeth fuse,
the jailers of words.

When there was nowhere to go,
nothing to hold,
he threw his limbs away,
simplifying his life.
He will not need his loins.
Wind blowing through the man
with a hole through his chest
won't turn him toward anyone.

The Lost Story

Then it was gone like
smoke: finding
a crack
in the hogan,
it expired
on the last breath.

The wind
scratches through a canyon
with a straw
picked up somewhere
among monoliths.

What a brave song it was.
There may have been
a coyote in it
who told an enemy's
secret. Surely a wing
feather of a god
who couldn't remain,
worn among silver
and turquoise;
and a maiden's half-joy
in the throes
of her knowledge of evening?

As when, in the breaking of clay,
two pieces are never
whole again, something is gone.

Or in the folding away
of the body, when we ask
ourselves, ashamed,
What is this untouchable
thing, present now
by a conspicuous vacancy?

Hitchhiker

Incensed by monoxide
I feel myself huddle within.
Wind on my bare knuckles falls
like a blow from the mace of winter,

and no-nonsense grandmothers,
righteous as swans,
are hoping to spy
from the corners of straight-ahead eyes,

the foot and a half of lead,
rolled in my *Daily Globe*,
that could pipe them off to sleep.
Or the secret power saw

(for trimming salesmen into blocks
of solid citizen)
that reposes in well-oiled parts
in my canvas overnight bag.

My God, I would sit for hours
in somebody's Volkswagen,
with a Doberman cocked like a .45
at the base of my only skull—

just to be moving
out of these everyday lives.

The Paper Route

All hair, The Hair was wading back
into his fen, one warty hand
around a blonde all skin except for fronds
diaphanously sketched. He was
the Nazi pilot who cracked up,
turned hirsute by the vapors of the swamp.
Those Sunday 3 A.M.'s
gave me half-hours for feasting eyes
in juicy comic strips.

Stars through the office window's patina of dust
went winking off. Meanwhile I sandwiched
brides and wars between Mandrake and Dick Tracy,
loading my fishmonger cart
till it could drag me down a hill,
its four-foot iron wheels rolling like tumbrils
through the empty town.

From under the stone cat squatting on a porch
I scooped the weekly change,
folded in a usual bread wrapper—mark of
the mystery subscriber.
For the lady in whose breath I reeled
weak as grasshoppers corked in empty pints,
I dropped a *World.*

Elks' Lodge, Old People's Home, dodging
a three-legged dog like a running stool.

Coffee and donuts building below the heart,
during church a stained-glass sunrise turned my sight
to tears. I prayed to printer's ink greasing my palms,
the fray of paper under fingernails,
asked for an arm like Christ's to reach
that third floor porch—
the paper drifted down in parachutes.

On the edge of town cows lowed. My nemesis,
the man with the umbrella,
phlegm dripping from his nose like Jack Frost's
icicle in thaw, turned from the cart as I came
through a yard. A paper clutched under his overcoat?
One *Advertiser* short, the last house
on the route would get a *Globe.*

And back in bed, The Aztec Queen,
indecently attired,
shot with me into sleep via outer space.

Paysage Moralise

The moon's own
daddy, they flopped
like rag dolls
into his arms.
Love wasn't rationed,
so he spread it thick.

Still, he was ravenous,

and like a wooden
marker in a childhood
game, he jumped
competitors
and scored.
It was always a bore,

and he never went sated.

Until one
midnight, when,
tracking his *ignis fatuus*
to conclusion,
into a grove the goat-boy clopped,
and spied

beside

her pool a rather
flat-chested naiad.
Creeping closer,
he found a dense
down feathered
her upper lip,

that she was lacking

in chin
and had a bulbous nose.
As he looked on, rapt,
the skinny nymph saddled
him, and water-eyed,
rode him like a stone

to the muddy bottom.

Appalachian Spring

A bad breath blows fog into the bag.
Night draws it shut

and Mail Pouch signs begin to sweat
the sides of rotting barns.

Someone's out nailing Risen Jesus ads
to roadside trees,

and busy clankings west of here
deliver coal caesarean. A tailgate

slams up the potholed street.
Invisible new tires spiel

through the Chevvy dealer's sleep.
His plucked-hawk look

crimps while the breakfast news
details the rape: headlights swath

the fog down a strip mine.
Shove of red tangled meat.

Call home when you get there,
the baby sitter's father

flashes her with steel-rimmed eyes.
He can't look me in the face tonight.

My Father Coming Home

1952

Canine, the face of the senator from Wisconsin
rises and comes on like a moon jowled blue
above the Mystic River's deadfall.

Under that sign my father
is leaning on the door of Gene's Cafe,
keeping chlorotic light from spilling
into the street. And now he is coming home
hand over hand up Reed Ave.'s chain link fences.

Soon we will shake again
with the clatter of Al Smith's train
entering Boston pumped full of home-loaded ammo,
the center of our history.

Because a son can take to probing
embalmed sharks at the kitchen table,
and another won't burn a ball off the house
on Saturday,
and a third plays in a box
and wears corrective glasses,
his fourth son tries to move
between second base and third
like the ghost of Marty Marion.

And because the Crash scared him a shade
of civil service gray,
in one summer month my father recovers color
by planting blueberries or trying
to grow a lawn on sand, these good frustrations
after a year of eight-hour days
of stretching one hour's work.

Under the moon out hunting scapegoats
for his life, he is coming home
where two sons can't drive nails or cars
and one's afraid of heights.
Come home, come home anyway, his sons are saying.
Though we won't be state troopers or toll collectors,
all will be trailed by the blue-jowled man
in the California moon,
and on certain nights we'll have to be prayed home
hand over hand.

For My Father, in the First Spring of His Passing

You would have liked today.
Sun piling through the grove
makes your white house
seem under sea.
Out on the marsh
a lone mallard skids in,
joining its shadow
among dragonflies.

It is not yet the time
for summer lightning,
when the air hangs heavy
with bristling words.
Tonight this place
will twang like a guitar.

Here is your chair, left out,
its wicker splayed with indirection,
stuff blowing off
like milkweed through the scrub.

Tamed to scrapbooks now,
you are a beery older pal
whose T-shirt bellies
like a spinnaker,
lolling beside me through
my puberty.

And when I carried you
to bed, thin as a stick man
crayoned by my son,
when finally I could cry
outside myself,
Save it for later,
that was all you said.

The one I drove past once in snow
far out the Newcastle road,
white, Victorian, a bare grove at its left side
like a hand upraised to dusk,

three stories slicing winds
that stream down off Lake Erie
and east across the flatness of Ohio.

These nights I keep returning
to rooms a lifetime shelters.
The foyer is that polished convent hall
where I awaited clicking beads
cold Saturdays,
                    collecting for my papers.

Except my father lives there now. Without his crutches,
no longer dying in a chair under a maple tree
while breezes click at fish and birds of glass.

Flanked by post office friends, in uniform,
he points the finger. He is melting from their arms
into the tiles, like wax.

Here is the yellow room I will not open.
I am not there, though in late afternoon
the sun falls in aslant the motes of dust.

Outside,
my footprints cross the snow, trek back
the way they came. Across the hall
an unmade bed, night shivering in a mirror.

I live under wide cellar beams, inhaling a dirt floor,
for years shouldering the past's footfall.
At one end, in a grove, I fish from a tall rock;
the hornpout sting

until my wife taps a low door
and lets me out.

My age
is like the field that unlit place stands in,
as if I stood beside the field,
looking through snow across stubbles of corn
to the far edge rimmed with a fusion of pines,
no longer a young view, and not the one I hope
from middle age.

After Midnight

In Kansas a shadow is moving
across one yellow square
of farmhouse window
into my sleep.
At a line behind his place
the stars leave off
and the earth comes in
from the horizon like a breeze,
keeping his floor and the phone
on his secondhand table
from joining the night
above those stars. In ringing
Connecticut I drop back
to the same earth
at the same time an hour older
and headlights are rolling
over and over like lanterns swung
on the road to Atchison.
Thin as a paper cup, metal quits,
and then, or now,
a woman is bleeding and someone
that might have isn't going to
live. Across 1,500 miles
tires, brake linings, the weave
of a prayer
fray with the recitation
of another year.

Waking

And that dream-mate stranger and father,
the polyhedral friend turned enemy,
whom you have been punching
without effect or pain, warps backward
into mist whose colors
some part of you prefers, folding himself
for easy storage, like a toy
set free of breath.

Or, if you have been dropping
past night-lights or a wall engraved
with pie-eyed fish and flowering mandibles,
you have bounced once in sleep without knowing it,
and the mattress has yielded its fit
to your shoulder and thigh again.
Now you may know that someone
is going to arrive or leave today, or an old
misunderstanding reappear.

If the last dream was good,—a woman or man you can't regain
by plowing back into the pillow, foliage that outdid
any October, or if you were dropping out of the sky
to land with one trampoline step
on the roof of a convertible, tipping a hand
to bystanders who recognized your grace
and spoke of it long after you had gone,—
getting up today may be an anticlimax,
as if in sleep you had said the perfect words,
the forgotten prayer which insures
the accessibility of anything.

For Theodore Roethke

In the first of a late June evening,
with a sudden litter of wings
and bristling penumbra of cold,
a butterfly or moth alighted, dun,

with spread antennae
like flower pistils,
a fuzzy, mottled burr.
Fearless with intelligence,

it was off across the garden
and back again and again
on my leg, knee, shoulder,
until, extending a finger

the way you offer a hand
to a strange but friendly hound,
I watched it carefully mount,
one foot at a time,

its inquisitive eyes
the color of sun
in old brown bottles.
Had he come? Had he finally become

that diminutive common thing?
Have it what way you will,
but for weeks I have flicked
horsefly and spider

and every meandering ant
gently onto the grass,
and for whole days
forgotten my bitterness.

Say your father came to a bad end
in a pie & you were
the only one of his kids
with a sensible name,
three goody-good sisters
called Flopsy, Mopsy, & Cottontail,
& every morning your mother
buttoned you up
in a blue blazer
& Mr. McGregor prepared
for your visit, ran water
into a pan
with a sound like voices
at somebody else's party,
strung up gooseberry nets
to catch your gold buttons in,
& kept a sieve handy for you,
spikes on his soles & heels;
& the mouse with the pea
in his mouth
was too busy hustling
for the family to tell you
a way out of the garden
so by the time you got home
your three sisters
had bread & milk & blackberries
for supper
while you gnawed the carrot
of desperation, waiting for a siren
like a new widow's lament
& your door kicked in
by official brown shoes—

then you would know
why even as a kid
though you felt you shouldn't have
you took Peter's side.

Bum

Feared wish or wished fear,
it was always there:
the spurious wallpaper flowers,
view of the harbor
you took for an image of freedom,
though you suspected it might be
a folding screen.
Driven there by a scar of words
that split you the way
lightning divides a tree,
it begins the day you run out
of a change of socks,
or a sleeve tears
on a corner of wall shadow,
the wife and kids by now
illustrations of parts
in a manual left by a previous tenant.
Your shoes complain
of necessities gone without,
until, like eccentric sisters,
they devise a running argument,
driving you into the street.
Then your electric gesturing,
light snapping along vertebrae,
exploding over the cerebellum.
Faceful of old newsprint
shouting What is this?
What is this?
into strangers' eyes.

Let's give it the Kamjian-Boyadjian Post,
Armenian-American War Vets,
and two bars with German names. Steuben's
and the Gartenhaus, say, with a drunk
whose face is sheer argument against shaving
emerging from under a torn convertible
roof and going into one or the other bar,
hands stuffed in a salt-and-pepper overcoat.
And scatter things around—
a few pebbles for leaping into shoes, and one
avocado ballpoint pen with pseudo-gold-metal trim
to be found by someone pretty coming home
from high school. We'll need a puddle
with a starling in it wading after sun,
and a Puerto Rican car with lacy dolls
and dingleberries in the rear window.
And paint "God-is-my-Co-pilot"
in flag colors across the right front fender.
Time for some people to come home from work:
have that clandestine couple arrive
separately and enter the Gartenhaus
one at a time; her first, leggy, with him
tearfully proud coming behind.
Red brick for these houses, or better yet
that yellow gravelly siding stamped
like brick. Never aluminum—who would
we fool with it? Or by calling it
Old Oaken Bucket Way? We'll call it
Soaper Street and add piles of fresh turf
in the Soaper Street Cemetery down one end beside
that padlocked store with what look like
used stove-parts in the window.

See that lady there being helped
by her remaining son? Her face
has stared down Death so many times
he's afraid to take her.

Rookie's Place

A quarter of your dollar and the jukebox
tells the story. Straight from a heart
cramped somewhere between vinyl boots and jaw
dislocated by a first husband,
she spins her tales of treachery and divorce.

The bongs and plinks of playpens amplified,
we know this music. Beyond its rainbow
strip mines multiply, and children
through whose cheekbones poverty shines
like watered sun.

Locals tight-eyed with spite,
the drunk tipped to one side
as if dragged by a hand squeezing his heart,
Ida Lupino in buckskin behind the bar,
and you and I, are waiting for The Cat Lady
whose earrings are the bottoms of tin cans.

Her tits hang like shotguns cradled,
and pop-tops chain her slippery waist.

With eyelids smeared like profiles
of fast cars,
she strafes the room and proves
the bangles of this music true:
we're all the slaves of love.

The Man in the Story

You were told to me one afternoon in the Elbo-Room
by a veteran of the place: the kind of man
you know is bad around children,
or has none, camel's-hair overcoat,
hound's-tooth hat, jumpy, cheeks falling to booze
like wizened apples.

He wheedled the bartender, who had a mean back
and a tongue like a sore waitress
and spent his shift trying to make patrons believe
they were invisible.

When Overcoat saw my books he told me about you:
merchant seaman who spent your off-hours at the typewriter
or reading. In his story you cry to yourself
and never go ashore,
but for fifteen years
you've been a profile of purpose,
a finger poised above the keyboard,
hunting letters.

Till now I never wondered about your face.
I've even thought that someone has a job
editing your life, papers and magazines
arriving with words blacked,
some country or woman the crew won't mention
in your presence.

You were a warning about books
from a drunk to me,
and I envied your free time
and that wall of words you built up on the page.

I didn't want to be successful Apple Cheeks,
who later tried to fight me anyhow,
and even less the bartender.
My daughter's crying from a minor hurt
I have to go look at. When I come back
be gone.

two

The Bats

Somebody said for killing one
you got a five-dollar reward
from Red Farrell the game warden,
because at night they drank cow blood,
dozens of them plastered on the cow
like leaves after a rain,
until she dropped.
If they bit you you'd get paralyzed for life,
and they built their nests
in women's hair, secreting goo
so you couldn't pull them out
and had to shave it off.
That was how Margaret Smith got bald,
though some said it was wine.
But who ever saw one
or could tell a bat from the swifts
they sometimes flew with,
homing on insects those green evenings?
We never climbed the fence of Duffy's orchard
to catch them dog-toothed
sucking on his pears,
and the trouble was, as Duffy always said,
that in the dark you couldn't
recognize them for the leaves
and might reach up and get bit.
So the first time one of us found one
dead and held it open,
it looked like something crucified
to a busted umbrella,
the ribbed wings like a crackpot would make
to try and fly off of a dune.

As if it was made up of parts
of different animals, it had long bird-legs
stuck in lizard wrinkle pants,
and wire feet.
It wasn't even black, but brown and furry
with a puppy nose,
and when we threw it at each other
it wouldn't stick on anyone.
Then someone said his father knew somebody
who used to hunt between town and the back shore.
Coming home one night he ran across
a bat tree in the woods,
must have been hundreds folded upside down
pealing their single bell-notes through the dark.

Enfield, Massachusetts

under Quabbin Reservoir

Water lets nothing mark it. So, if you need
a preconceived direction, you can troll
down the laid-out streets.
7,000 souls transplanted with their stones.
But, in the knowledge that human work
is always partly done, a few bones go
uncollected. Think of a clavicle or two,
an ulna, nothing heavily sunken.
In the steady lean of inland tide
they are turning over, slow-motion parodies
of straws in a wind.
Trolling, lures hook and hang
on the snaggled teeth of a fence,
a lunatic bug collection. Bass coming home
won't close the gate, or keep the path
in deference to the lawn, ignore your shadow,
your rowing on the sky.

The Camels

You cannot say
that on the sixth
morning they will appear,
on the tenth day
a perforation of space,
at an indefinable distance,
will begin.
For they are the beasts
whose rabbit faces
are singed with knowledge,
whose necks insinuate
music wheedled
from slow pipes.
On feet like the plates
of mine detectors
they are coming at their pace
over what may be the same ground
volleyed forward and back
in the ignorant wind.
Rags stringing bone to bone,
the men with them
are walking the years
of their lives
on unmeasuring feet.
And while you wait
they are bringing
no understandable news
but the sweat of the earth.

Dog

I

Odor of some other life
drifts from his back: of fog
invading low places near the sea,
grass turning a wet bronze,
shell-flake, a blue rowboat
anchored to its reflection.

II

Set your palm on the skull,
roofed sleek as a shark's.

Hooded teeth welcome your fist.
Sometime he has been among wolves,

or an old sire turned aside
in a long procession of yaks,
and lay in a field
becoming a stone of silence,

mountain winds
combing his horns into dust.

That could explain this shag.

III

I too twitch in sleep,
remembering other lives.
I remember a man who would chew glass
if you bought him a beer
to wash it down.

And I have climbed out the end
of drunken limbs myself,
though I say I love the color green.
This dog is my ragged shadow.

IV

Dog, I want your patience.
To sit and do nothing
without this jiggling foot.
Where did you earn your quiet?
I want to go there.
Speak.

Crows

Raucous as baseball fans
in the grandstand
of summer, masked band
of country brigands,
they slide from morning's air
on serrated black hands,
a goofy mafia
sporting comic-crooked stares,
come to play havoc with
the simmering garbage pit
under the pines.

Darker than dark, dark leaves
them undefined.
Their bad report
rackets about the eaves,
moiling the deep
cool eddies of our sleep.
They've got the goods
on us. The worst we fear
is true:
they are here for more than sport.

Heron

A white feather
hangs like a pen
from a clerk's
ear, and his
clerk's eye,
his whole
profile, aims
for the final
pronouncement of
black beak.

He hunches because
he has willed
himself down
through the bamboo
of his legs.

He reflects
for hours
on himself.

Until, for a
flash
in his dark
undergut,
he smashes
himself dead
center, a flotsam
of blue and white
feathers.

Looking up, he flips
a silverside
to his working
throat.

When he looks down
a target of blue
and white
will melt
into its center.

The Invisible Animal

Awake to the July moon
over a woman's flesh, I have heard you
stamp the earth before a place
I rented with whiskey.
What did you spare me of?
Your crown of bone?
You could have had her—
I with no weapons but fly rods.

Where did I first feel
your hidden breath on my back?
On the sun-burning trail
to Great Pond, where a hush
from shuddering scrub
sent me hot-footed home
without an excuse for my father?

I have looked long into leaves
for a sight from the shade,
for a snout darker than shadow.

Is your breath a benediction,
or the smack of a feral lip
attuned with the rustle of oaks?
Do yellow pupils register,
then cancel us
from an unconcerning brain?
Or are you fleet
as a night pond over skin?

Proposals Made in the Name of Reason

Of the paranoia of supermarkets,
the sonic boom shuddering the umbilicus,
rainbows collapsed on rivers of grit,
acknowledge your fears.
Avoid the midnight light of gas stations:
where the sludge of engines is poured
nothing can grow.

*

Before there are woodchucks
whose entrails smoke with heat of decibels,
let us no longer patronize the earth.
Uncapitalize all Nature;
not dreaming of abstract trees,
but watching the blue smoulder
of certain pines.

*

For what they have done,
invented the rain of acid, the toy
no fungus can yet return to soil,
there may be men who deserve
to spin bumbling out of fires.

*

Bashful before common things,
the burdock and pigweed, anemone, godwit
and scoter, the young who bend to each other
the springing reeds of their bodies,
return to earth dominion
over the risen dust of all its creatures.

*

With arms opened wide as water
praise earth's secret face.

three

Why 135 Vials of Blood Are Missing from General Hospital

Imagine a girl who wore flat-fronted
maroon uniforms with white scalloped collars
and maroon knee socks, schooled by nuns
so long she felt like a buoy assaulted by flotillas.
During technician school she spent so many nights
before the TV that its blue light leached her pigment.
She once sneaked a panatella of Daddy's, she was
that suggestible to commercials, and while she
dreams of doctors the popcorn is working its way
from her feet up her thickening ankles.
Three a day for forty-five days,
she secretes the vials in her purse, and upstairs
where Teddy Bear questions her dyeing a sheet
she's been keeping under the bed.
High on the hemoglobin of her moment,
at the Employee's Masquerade
her false eyelashes butterfly out of their slits.
Red leotards swell from her toes
like a vertical kiss.

Bear at the Academy of the Living Arts

Got there early.

Women the color of preserved baby shoes
kept trying to knock Bear down
with their big eyelashes.
Athens, says one. *Rome,* argues another.

They were blowing
up the president of the Academy.
Bicycle pump in his belly button.

More air to the bow tie, said the lady
with big glasses on.

He's very high-powered, she said to Bear.
What do you do?

Big eyes, she had.
Bear kept his hands at sides.
Organs collapsed inside.

Rub my ass on trees? Can't tell her that,
                              Bear thought.

Eat blueberries and sleep? Nix on that, too.

Bite the hand, Bear said. *Feeds me.*
Oops. Slipped out. Bear's hand over mouth too late.

What they call you? asked she,
                              smile all hung out.

Stud, Bear lied.
Stub, laughed she, *tha's cute.*

Bear came by, sat down.
Invited, of course.

Misterwriter not there yet.
Misterwriter not here yet, said Missiswriter.
She's kind of nice, Bear thought. *Bad legs tho'.*
Like chickens'.

Missiswriter went out the door.
Misterwriter, she yells. *Bear here!*

No answer. She yells again.

No answer.

Misterwriter comes in other door.
Sees me, Bear thinks, *but he's making believe.*

Misterwriter looks around, talking to self.
Bumps into table. Goes to spot marked X.

Missiswriter comes in. *There!* to Misterwriter.
He turns, discovers Bear on sofa.

Hellooo! Hand out.

*   *   *

Know all the constellations now, said Misterwriter,
Rigelgoose,
Betelgaff,
Glattstop.

Glattstop, Bear marveled, *that's hard.*

Not so, said Misterwriter.

No, of course, Bear said. *Try to be nice,*
Bear thought.

Tough, though. This time of year, Misterwriter said.

Really? said Bear.

Of course, said Misterwriter. *Too low.*
On the horizon.

Really? said Bear.

Of course!

Change the subject, Bear thought. *What's that for? Insulation?*
Soundproofing?

Haaaa! Haaaa! laughed Misterwriter. *What could it be for?*

How do I know? Bear replied. Thinking: *Do I have a bucket on my foot?*
My wife made it, said Misterwriter.

*   *   *

If I like him, Bear asked himself, going home, *why did I wave good-bye*
with both hands?

Noun

"How do we inspire students to love the printed word?"

Here is the word *noun* printed in Lydian Cursive.
Think of that older woman
who sits in front of you
in Psych. 21. But think of her ebb and flow
on the chaise lounge up at her place,
in something comfortable,
after about two quarts
of Boone's Farm Wild Strawberry.

Now note the pneumatic uplift
of those N's, one for each hand;
the together slowness of your fingertips
tracing her O. Can you dig
the goblet of her U?

N stands for knob,
and what a pair
for dialing yourself in on!
If you're man enough
you can slip through that O
into womb-blue midnight,
a Milky Way of motivating stars.

But just in case money's your bag,
here is a verb in Bank Script,
glowering on a legal letterhead
above foreclosures. More
about this next time, and making
quick conjunctions,
and how to manipulate adverbs
to your advantage.

Thunderstorm, Cape St. Vincent

It is the air shot through
with green silk.

It is God
rambling blind drunk on ozone,
each planted foot
shocking Himself awake.

And yes, it is angels
fighting it out with no. 9 irons
across the heavenly links,
it is all these and more because now
is no time for good reasons.

The sun cannot win.
Trees try to get up and go.
Leaf to leaf, foot soldiers of the rain . . .

A man may watch the rain
fleer off his eaves,
smoke of his pipe updrafting,
but a struck woman wears black
from that day on,
and no longer goes
to pick hillside dandelions.

The young girls put shakers of salt
on the opened Book of Isaiah.
They leave two doors ajar
and skip into closets,
waiting with tensed lashes,
with crossed arms.
Let it take what it wants and go.

Unfishing

Once each August I meet my brother
in the harbor parking lot. We get together
other times, I like him maybe because
when both of us were smaller
I dropped him with a punch
he's never tried to avenge.

The day hangs a blue haze,
water's so flat you could float a dime on it.
When the two horses clank *I won't, I won't,*
after forty pulls, "Maybe someday one of us
will have something that works," he says,
while I curse British Seagull Motors, Ltd.,
and row for an invisible X
a quarter mile straight north of the jetty blinker,
close enough to swim for it if the skiff springs
a strake.

No gulls or terns are flinging down on bait
like desperate gloves, and no boats circle
with men twitching rods in the Deep's face.
It's too warm here for anything but crabs.

My pole I bought for brook trout the summer I was fifteen.
It retrieves a barbless plug cut from a broom handle,
a motion like nothing in water anywhere.

Fishing for more than blues or even stripers,
but trying not to jerk a hook through anything,
he asks how come I never went into business.

The Wise Owl Bar

The Wise Owl Bar
is a parking lot for
Bluebonnet Banquets now.
A wedding party limo
can slip its shine
through the front door
without spilling a drop
or customer to mar
its simonize. It's
empty as Sunday morning:
the 1 A.M. truck brake
like gas from a drowned
dog snaps nobody awake
in a rear booth, and
nobody blowing the head
off his glass of snow
is watching out the window
beer falling on
the Mt. Holyoke Range.

Native American Opera

Somehow the woman has been with child
three years. She holds a hand there
wondering how, giving the room a pregnant look
while the organ, always pregnant, swells violently.
The season is indoors, the state Catatonia.
There, while snow, dust, and raised eyebrows fall,
a hand moves over a table, slow as a man on all fours
crossing a desert. Later it covers another hand,
symbiotically. Then there's a shattered windshield,
or inexplicable headaches, and somebody who left town
comes back with another face, but no one will notice,
only the audience crying Look out! Look out!
That's not your son! until swaddled in small talk.
Drinks swirl all the time, clicking the ice,
but no one falls down or throws up on his lawyer's suit.
A lady is told her father isn't her father.
Mascara runs. When the child is born
it's already six months old.

four

Fifty miles down the road you can give
five bucks to some guy
with a thread-riddled nose
like a road map of Vermont
and get a symmetrical tree.
Not me. Third-growth pine
is best, where sand farmers have failed
and where it was recut
to fire a tryworks in whaling days.
A broken puzzle of snow on the ground,
wear a coat long enough to bootleg in
a saw. This bottom was Ned
McLaughlin's, those mounds
are where he spaded his dead
horses. Look close
and you might see a wicket of ribs
stick up like a rotting skiff.
Now look for a tree
whose northeast side isn't flat
with wind off Georges Bank.
Be sure to top it high and light enough
so you can drag it back. Keep off the roads,
or if you really have to move,
being seen, balance it easily over
one shoulder. It's more than likely
once you set it up you'll see the top
won't point, but forks,
imperfect as a life, no pinnacle
for an angel. A green bow
and a chocolate Santa Claus
dressed in red foil will camouflage
that gray spot on the trunk.

Now plug it in, no talk of ritual,
get out the bourbon (each sip's
Christmas Eve), and rinse a glass clean
for the chief of police.

Ward's Grove

I

Ward won't see it. Just like he'd never seen
Miami Beach, so sold this place I used to climb in

trying to reach a high green star or dream back
to the last wolf in the territory.

He said, "We don't amount to a piss-hole in the snow,"
and claimed to hoe a little fog on winter mornings.

Brim down and collar up, he made some of the paths
I used to follow. All over town

they wound like life lines on his hands,
around bases of hogsbacks, picking up and dropping

the double sand track of the Old King's Highway.
A peeping tom, some said, that's why he kept off roads.

Ward's gone to Florida, so he won't see
the oil derrick offshore like Triton's middle finger.

II

He built his place alone, tarred trunks I skinned
with a dull hatchet, and kicked the traps I set

lopsided. Behind his Hen Hop Inn
he'd scrape and paint a double-ended dory

white and clean-lined as the church
he swore that only Death would catch him dead in.

He's far enough not to hear the seventeen-year locust
of the chainsaw. Far enough so I can't blame him.

III

Who do I blame? My aunts, who could have had this grove
for sixty dollars, but wouldn't go a snicker

over forty-five? The realtor who says sound rises,
that these cheeseboxes are the logical extension

of the saltbox? Town Fathers who believe it?
Where is the sparrow Ward named Blue, who took seeds

off his palm? Blueberries retire around the swamp
dredged for tame fish, and Ward's coop tinted silver

lines the inside of a piano bar. He's gone
to Florida and up three lanes Florida comes here.

The Snow

Something, a withheld immensity,
predicted the day would end.
Someone knocking off work
dropped a board, a clap
shoving itself through air,
interrupting an erratic tick
in oak leaves. Simple,
quiet as lichens,
flakes sift down,
mapping the creature trails,
leaning into everything:
a common ground, a vacancy
emptying this room,
nowhere everywhere.

Inversions of Summer

As though a shell drew in
its mother-of-pearl,
light recedes.
Battened and low,

clouds set sail.
Mistrals arise
where summer dissolved
a world's extremities.

Dunes marble,
and the last pastel
falls on old snow
as on a drove of sheep.

Pity the unregenerate
of memory, when this diminished
land fails the Atlantic.
All day I have winnowed

in the chaff of summer.
Nine hoary tufts on
nine spiles are the story
of geese that rode the flood

at Scorton's Creek.
Blue pines shudder
and bundle, and something
in the summerhouse

will not give up its breath.
The crow knows this:
who lack a mind's eye
are too small a word.

Then he invented the running wolf behind the wind,
the rifle barrel edged from frozen bushes,
stories for turning sluggish ropes of blood,

reddening the rorschach in his heart's
salt cave. For courage he recalled
the inchworm going home,

high in the glow of summer dusk,
two hundred forty times above itself.
His forehead slicked with dross

of the distilling blood.
He felt his eye roam clear,
drink in the afternoon:

the amber sun, the low hills afterthoughts
between the sea and sky,
ice locked in ringed panes

like the years of trees.
In loose flocks, evening grosbeaks
flung out of their branches,

yellow flags a summer had left over.
Then he was running where
pines dipped their shadows in a sluice

of water. Slowing to walk against the wind
he let slip through his fingers,
as quiet as the time, time entered in:

the orange, thumbnail tip of sun
and last fruits of day: eelgrass softening
from tan to plum:

sky going down on fire
behind an island: the purpling sea:
sky citrus, pear, then empty of these lights.

Stranger,

this morning while you reckoned the figures up
I took a walk over Tom's Hill Road
to the harbor; with only a freckling
of wind the last wisps of tide ebbed
in the bight, exposing the sea's underpinning,
the shell-spattered muck of moon snails
and periwinkles, barnacle crops
on water-soft wood, and those
pronged, riven bulbs that house before life
the skate fish.
           And this is my place:
there is no tax on the uncounted legs
of the sea worm. Though all night
my wife may stick by my side
while I murder friends in a sweat
for their small change, you will not
learn it from me, or our pet names for each other
or our mutual needs; nor any moral
or new proof of divinity.
Beyond your numbers
I see a radish climb out of its crater.
Look. All over the earth is
opening little graves.

Blackfish Creek

Far in the mellow deep of summer, off four round ponds strung north,
the long still-stand of ice flows through pine breath,
emanation of glacial memory jousting with dwarf pines.
Slow trickle of sand down pond scarp. A half mile out,
gulls roost or rise, hunting the shore for mussels.

Head slick as an eight ball,
our bowlegged uncle
in ice-cream trousers
smiled beneath rimless glasses,
doling hard candy from a jar
in his maroon Studebaker.
Our pants rolled to the knees,
we walked behind him croaking,
Old uncle Bill!   Old uncle Bill!
Aunt Mary's pen idealized
scavenging gulls and crows.
Who will answer the bobwhite now?

Yard by yard, two thousand years of sand curls south, fattening Monomoy.
At Blackfish Creek the spring tide runs up the hanging valley,
homing the scarp and berm to the Atlantic, swamping the white cedar
                                        where the catbird cries.
Broken the vessel of memory, the images vestigial as wisps of sand isle.
                                        Two thousand years.
By the forsythia, quail pore in the unmowed grasses.
                        White clapboards bleach in the salt sun.

Long Pond Summer

Dawn creeping gray from offshore
scattered the ducks beelining
across the water.

Each needle bled its pine droplet
of sun and sent squirrels tattering
over the tarpaper roof.

Some mornings
you woke to a dream
of the snout of a wayfaring hound

outside your screen.
A skreak of the cast-iron pump
and from under all Wellfleet

the gurgling of ferrous water rose up
and the day began. Through
the bellicose howls of kids

in love with a sinking float,
you thought of the tired clump
of fur and claw in the road,

and wrote a poem ending in 'strange'. Selling
air-conditioned meat
to bronzed New Jersey matrons,

leaning close you bartered with your lust.
Outside the cicadas sang *heat.*
And in evenings green as apples,

home to the driftwood fire;
in the devil-glare redness of lobster,
a girl slipping off her white sweater,

like the moon coming up on long water.

The Salt Farm

Only a woman out foraging
for beach plums or blue-eyed grass
could have found this place
up the old railroad embankment,
beyond where someone with a .22
danced a Coca-Cola can up the trail
till it turned to a sieve.

A cottontail bobs around the bend
above us, on a path crisscrossed with fox runs
and the fetor of skunk, lined with cinders,
and railroad ties, their marrow gone.

In a glacier-made kettle hole out of the wind,
below an inverted bowl of sky an occasional gull inscribes,
or a sparrow hawk crying its *killy killy*
over a shrew on the headland, she noticed first
the alien blue spruce, planted maybe to frame the house,
though there is no cellar hole.

                    Then she saw the kitchen midden
and among bushes the rotten fence post, wire and its tunes
long since run off with the wind, and the garden green
even in August, but grown to marshy hardhack.

A crab apple life, with peat and loam hauled in for the momentary
defeat of sand, the cows ruminating on salt hay against the sky,
outhouse halfway up the hill where a fresh wind could get it.
No sea view, but a practical love must have known
how whipped brine hardens a woman's looks, how distances
detract from the matter at hand.

                    Only on a bad day
could they realize the sound big water makes, but here
in the foggy dark must have been like life
on the floor of a pond.

Is it failure without a name, or only that where nothing is wasted
wood gets carted off for someone else's warmth,
that brings us close against the earth's foreclosure?

The Last Day of October

The last summer complaint has cranked his hull
out of the harbor.
Gulls stand by like cold monsignors
while the tides clear of outboard fuel.

Already twice my age, white paintflake
from her August blistering, pastel-smudged
from prams she's shouldered,
this dory may outlast my brushwork and brass screws:
a floorboard still floats in last week's rain.

Birdshot across Tom's Hill.
In the mind's eye a pheasant escapes
on creaking hinges.

Near turning, the current dies,
slack as a sail in horse latitudes.
A hovering kingfisher squawks,
dives, blue bullet hunting the river's heart.

Thousands of elvers move like filings in a force field,
squirming crosscurrent,
sidling together where the tide flushes
tumbleweeds of kelp.

Coming around, the bow points downstream:
brown feathers sculling toward the finished year,
a solitary loon.

Getting Back Into the Country

I

A piece at a time,
some selfish machine is breaking down
in its deep-fried air.
Hums diminish,
one after another fans evolve into blades.
The spark plugs crack like fossils of dragonflies;
mechanics of squeak and grind
feed their repair kits
to oxidizing fields:
the ear arrives.

II

Though even the water's horizon is choppy,
and clouds evangelically glow
in their separate shapes,
though trees warp, trying for insignificance,
spelling out nothing, with nothing to sell,
my eyes stretch at distances,
pain for the sharps and flats
of vertical arrangements,
peripheral blinders.

III

Deer pass in a dream.
I step out into the air.

I believe I could cure the blind
with a cup of this wind.

In the Hour of Quiet

Whimbrel, brown creeper, windflower:
in the hour of quiet I name nonhuman things,
inventing a few for myself alone:
hawk-willow, devil's kiss, smokeweed.

Ideally it's when the moon stalls
in midwinter branches, and home
is a house I'm by myself in.

I hear my blood jump in its rapids,
and listen for it
dropping the slow falls
the way I imagine the dead listen.

These times I go into lost places,
a grove deep in childhood
where peripheral houses shrink
to moths against a screen,

or a field I've never seen
high up some mountain, in which
a piece of hand-forged iron rusts,
that I can't place a use for.

I know the wind and more
is beating down the centuries,
and while I sit the tides go on
rearranging the earth.

Windflower, I whisper, who has never
seen one, weighing the risk of saying nothing
against the risk of being a fool.

The pump squats in the cellar
like a troll, grousing through bad teeth
about its work.

Somewhere in the hour's parenthesis
a towhee scuffles leaves.

In a voice that's three parts rain
a word escapes the dead.

PITT POETRY SERIES